FAITH OPENS THE DOOR
TO THE SUPERNATURAL

Mark Hankins

FAITH OPENS THE DOOR
TO THE SUPERNATURAL
Mark Hankins

Unless otherwise indicated, all scriptural quotations are from the King James Version of the Bible.

Quotations of Smith Wigglesworth are taken from "Ever Increasing Faith," Wayne E, Warner, ed. Revised ed. (Springfield, MO: Gospel Publishing House, 1971.)

Some quotations are the author's paraphrase.

Faith Opens the Door to the Supernatural

ISBN # 9781889981536

First Edition 2016

Published By

MHM Publications

P.O. Box 12863

Alexandria, LA 71315

www.markhankins.org

Printed in the United States of America.

Table of Contents

The moment you act

on the Word of God,

God makes Himself

responsible

for your results!

1

FAITH IS MOTION ACTIVATED

CHAPTER ONE

I remember the first time I went into an airport bathroom where the water faucets were motion activated. I stood there looking for a handle or a pedal or something to turn the water on. I could not understand how this faucet worked. I thought, "We have a serious problem here; I don't know what their budget was, but someone has made a major mistake." It looked like the plumbing and the sinks were there, but there were no handles. While I stood there trying to figure this out, a man walked into the restroom and waved his hand under the water faucet. Immediately water began to come out. I thought I had just seen a miracle. Nonchalantly, the same man walked to the towel dispenser and began waving his hands under it in the same manner, and the towels came out. It was then I noticed a sign on the wall that read, "Equipment is motion activated."

As soon as I saw that sign, I began to think the same thing is true about faith. Faith is motion activated. In other words, God said, "Salvation is here, healing is here, deliverance is here and I am just waiting for someone to act in faith." While you are praising, rejoicing and dancing around, the water starts coming. Salvation, healing, and deliverance begin to come — they are motion activated.

One act of faith will open up the supernatural and cause the glory of God to come in. Jesus said in John 11:40, "...if thou wouldest believe, thou shouldest see the glory of God."

> *...Didn't I tell you that if you believed, you would see the glory of God?*
> *-John 11:40, Message*

BELIEVE IS A VERB

I recently watched a guy on television who said he had written the first novel which contained no verbs. He explained it was full of nouns, adjectives, pronouns and prepositions, but no verbs. The interviewers asked him how the book was selling, to which he replied, "not very well." When asked why, he simply said, "because it has no action."

The word "believe" is a verb and verbs always denote action. Faith, on the other hand, is a noun. Effective faith, faith that gets results, must be translated into action.

So also faith, if it does not have works (deeds and actions of obedience to back it up), by itself is destitute of power (inoperative dead).
-James 2:17, Amplified

For as the human body apart from the spirit is lifeless, so faith apart from [its] works of obedience is also dead.
-James 2:26, Amplified

In my college psychology class, we learned that reasoning will not change an emotion, but action will. In other words, you cannot *feel* your way into better behavior, but you can *behave* your way into better feelings. God created us in such a manner where our actions are stronger than our feelings. Faith is an act. By faith we access the grace of God. Just a little bit of faith can access a whole lot of grace.

God has already done everything He is going to do about our salvation, our healing, our deliverance, and our blessing. Jesus paid it all. Then, He sat down. Now it is our move — we have to know what He's done for us and act in faith on the Word of God.

Many churches are full of nouns, adjectives, pronouns, and prepositions, but God is looking for verbs. He is looking for people who will believe and act in faith. Faith is what pleases God. Hebrews 11:6 says, "But without faith it is impossible to please God...."

FAITH THAT MOVES MOUNTAINS

Faith moves God and faith moves mountains. However, faith will not move anything until it moves you. The first part of you that your faith will move is your mouth. The moment you act on the Word of

God, He makes Himself responsible for your results.

Jesus said to him, If thou canst believe, all things are possible to him that believeth.

-Mark 9:23

Grace is God's grip on you.

Faith is your grip on God.

God's grip on you is greater

than your grip on Him.

2

THE RELATIONSHIP BETWEEN GRACE AND FAITH

CHAPTER TWO

By whom also we have access by faith into this grace wherein we stand, and rejoice in hope of the glory of God. -Romans 5:2

Grace is God's grip on you. Faith is your grip on God. God's grip on you is greater than your grip on Him. The Apostle Paul said, "Not as though I had already attained, either were already perfect: but I follow after, if that I may apprehend that for which also I am apprehended of Christ Jesus," Philippians 3:12. One translation says, "I have not yet gotten a hold of what has gotten a hold of me."

The reason faith is so important is because our faith gives us access to God's grace. When my kids were little and we would walk across a busy street, I would tell them to hold my hand. While they were holding my hand, I was holding theirs, but my grip on them was much stronger than their grip on me. They thought they were holding my hand, but in reality, I was holding theirs.

Romans 5:17 says, "For if by one man's offence death reigned by one; much more they which receive abundance of grace and of the gift of righteousness shall reign in life by one, Jesus Christ." God's abundant grace is what He has done for us in Christ. Faith is our response and acting on that abundant grace. One translation of Romans 5:17 says, "God's work in Christ far exceeds any damage done to us by Adam's fall."

As we can see in Romans 5:17-21, what God has done in Christ is greater than what satan has done in Adam. Grace shows us who we are in Christ. We see ourselves through the blood of Jesus and through the power of redemption in Christ. By faith we access that grace and hold fast to our confession of who we are in Christ.

*For by grace are ye saved through faith; and
that not of yourselves: it is the gift of God:
-Ephesians 2:8*

Again, we see the relationship between grace and
faith. All of God's grace is accessed by faith. The
Lord said to me, "You can steal information, but
you cannot steal revelation." God Himself opens
revelation to each believer and that is why we pray the
prayer in Ephesians 1:17-23. God's kingdom system
has never been "hacked." We use the word hacked
because the greatest businesses in the world make extra
efforts to keep their computer systems and information
from being broken into by cyber criminals. But no
matter how secure the world tries to make its system of
information, there is always someone who can break
into it. God's kingdom system, unlike the world's, has
never been and will never be hacked. If you got in, you
were granted access. The moment you are granted
access, there is a "download" of God's goodness,
God's mercy, God's grace, God's provision, and God's
wisdom. One of my favorite scriptures is Ephesians 3:12
which states, "In whom we have boldness and access
with confidence by the faith of him." So in Christ we
are granted access into God's kingdom system.

Your celebration is a
demonstration of
your expectation.

3

THE POWER
OF POSITIVE
EXPECTATION

CHAPTER THREE

My soul, wait thou only on God; for my
expectation is from Him. -*Psalm 62:5*

While watching a college football game, the team I was watching broke from their huddle and lined up for the next play. Everything looked normal until I noticed the quarterback had misjudged his position and was lined up behind the guard rather than positioning himself behind the center. When he called the play, nothing happened. I laughed as he looked up, saw his mistake, and made one step to the side. Upon the correction, the center released the ball into the quarterback's hands and the play was executed. Just as in that football game, sometimes we need to make adjustments in our expectation in order to receive answers to prayer. It is then that we will see great things accomplished for God.

In Psalm 42:5, David spoke to his soul, "Why art thou cast down, O my soul? And why art thou disquieted within me? Hope thou in God." Hope is an expectation of good and is a valuable ingredient in faith.

There are four kinds of expectation: negative, misguided, neutral and positive. It would be good to check up on yours to see that it is positive.

1. **Negative expectation** can be seen in the reaction of a guy whose friends put Limburger cheese under his nose while he was sleeping. When he awoke, he went from room to room looking to find the source of the smell. Finally, he went outside, took a deep breath and smelled the same odor. In disgust he said, "The whole world stinks!" In other words, he had a general attitude of negativity.

2. **Neutral expectation** is when our expectation never gets out of "neutral." Some people never decide to act upon the Word of God spoken to them or make any changes in their lives. "Some day" never comes and they find themselves stuck in the same place year after year.

3. **Misguided expectation** is like when Naaman expected Elisha to wave his hand over him to make his leprosy disappear. Instead, Naaman had to humble himself and dip seven times in the muddy river as instructed. Like Naaman, who was offended at the prophet's instructions, we may need to make adjustments, swallow our pride and obey the Word of the Lord in order to get a miracle.

4. **Positive expectation** is like the woman in Mark 5 who suffered for twelve years with an issue of blood. When she heard of Jesus, she pressed through the crowd behind Him, and touched His garment. She said, *"If I may but touch his clothes, I shall be made whole."* And *straightway the fountain of her blood was dried up; and*

she felt in her body that she was healed of that plague. And Jesus, immediately knowing in himself that virtue had gone out of him, turned him about in the press, and said, "Who touched my clothes?" But the woman fearing and trembling, knowing what was done in her, came and fell down before him, and told him all the truth. And he said unto her, "Daughter, thy faith hath made thee whole; go in peace and be made whole of thy plague," (Mark 5:27-34). This woman had a positive expectation, her faith was in God, and she got her miracle. When she said what she expected out loud, she also began to "see what she expected." She expected to be healed. She expected her next twelve years would not be like her last twelve years. **Positive expectation brings positive results.**

PAINT THE PICTURE ON
THE CANVAS OF YOUR MIND

When it seemed as though Jacob was limited by his circumstances, he opened the door to the supernatural. He allowed the Holy Spirit to paint the picture of the Word of God on the canvas of his heart.

In Genesis 30 and 31 we see that Jacob constructed a fence which cast a spotted and speckled reflection on the water where the cattle came to drink and to mate. His dream and corresponding action physically affected his cattle. This is faith that has works; it will change your family and your future. This kind of faith will cause you to fulfill God's plan for your life.

Ask God to give you the spirit of wisdom and revelation, to open the eyes of your heart. Sit before the Word of God and allow the Holy Spirit to paint the picture of His Word on the canvas of your heart. As Dr. Yonggi Cho said, "Dreams and visions are the language of the Holy Spirit."[1] *The Holy Spirit will take the things of Christ and help you translate them into personal victory!*

YOUR CELEBRATION IS A DEMONSTRATION OF YOUR EXPECTATION

Psalm 119:162 says, "I rejoice at thy word, as one that findeth great spoil." I like to say, "Your celebration is a demonstration of your expectation!" 1 Peter 1:8-9 says, "Whom having not seen, ye love; in whom, though now ye see him not, yet believing, ye rejoice with joy unspeakable and full of glory: Receiving the end of your faith, even the salvation of your souls." Your positive expectation, mixed with joy, is an important key to receiving from God. ***Joy is the bridge between believing and receiving.***

When Jesus was teaching,
He was never working on
the "giving" part of God,
He was always working on
the "receiving" part of man.

4

HOW YOU CAN RECEIVE ANYTHING FROM GOD

CHAPTER FOUR

Recently, I read an article in which Warren Buffet, a multi-billionaire, was asked his secrets to success. I thought he would share investment insights and strategies, but to my surprise, the two keys he attributed to his success were not related to finances. He said the first key to his success was his certainty of the unconditional love of his father. This certainty gave him great confidence in life and he was never afraid to attempt great things, nor was he afraid of failing.

The second key to his success was his discovery that he did not follow directions well. Learning to follow instructions was important for his success. He then gave an example of taking a test in school. The first words at the top of the test instructed him to write his name. The instructions then said to read every question on the test before answering any of them. Buffet wrote his name and began answering the questions. After one minute, a girl in the class stood up and turned in her test. Warren Buffet knew he was as smart as that girl and wondered how she had finished the test before him, but he continued to answer the questions. When he got to the very last question, it instructed him not to answer any of the questions, but rather to turn the test in to the teacher. Mr. Buffet said this taught him, as a boy, the importance of listening and following instructions.

I noticed the pilots who fly our ministry airplane have a checklist they follow for each take-off and landing. These are the same written, basic instructions they have gone over many times. I asked one of the older pilots why he went over the same simple written list each time he flew. He replied quickly, "Only a fool trusts his memory when his life is at stake." I told him, "That's why Jesus said, 'It is written!'"

The Word of God contains the written, unchanging procedures and steps to victory in every area of life. In order to get the results we want, we must go back over the basics of what Jesus taught. For the best results we must continue to review and practice these basic steps of faith.

There would have been no need for Jesus to teach if everything was sovereignly up to God. Jesus was teaching because we have a part to play in receiving. When Jesus was teaching, He was never working on the "giving" part of God, He was always working on the "receiving" part of man. He was helping us receive from God. You never have to talk God into healing anyone — He is the healer.

FOLLOW THE STEPS JESUS TAUGHT

> *Jesus said, "If anybody, anywhere, will take these four steps or put these four principles into operation, he will always receive, not only healing, but whatever he wants from Me or from God, the Father."*
> *-Rev. Kenneth E. Hagin*

Rev. Kenneth E. Hagin (Dad Hagin) tells of a visitation he had from the Lord Jesus where he asked Him about the healing of the woman who touched

Jesus' clothes in Mark 5. He told the Lord it seemed like there was more to this message than he had been preaching. Jesus simply answered him, yes, there was more. He told him to get a pen and paper and to write down the numbers 1, 2, 3, and 4. Jesus proceeded to give Dad Hagin the exact steps of faith the woman with an issue of blood took in order to receive her healing. He said, "If anybody, anywhere, will take these four steps or put these four principles into operation, he will always receive, not only healing, but whatever he wants from Me or from God the Father." I believe the Holy Spirit wants to remind us of these steps of faith so that we can see great results than ever before.

> *And a certain woman, which had an issue of blood twelve years, and had suffered many things of many physicians, and had spent all she had and was nothing bettered, but rather grew worse; when she heard of Jesus, came in the press behind and touched His garments. For she said, If I may touch but his clothes, I shall be whole. And straightway the fountain of her blood was dried up; and she felt in her body that she was healed of that plague. And Jesus, immediately knowing in himself that virtue had*

gone out of him, turned him about in the press, and said, Who touched my clothes?... And he looked round about to see her that had done this thing. But the woman fearing and trembling, knowing what was done in her, came and fell down before him, and told him all the truth. And he said unto her, Daughter, thy faith hath made thee whole; go in peace, and be whole of thy plague. -Mark 5:25-34

FOLLOW THESE INSTRUCTIONS

In this story Jesus told the woman, *"Daughter, your faith has made you whole."* What were the things she did? How did she exercise her faith? Jesus told Dad Hagin that this woman did four things which enabled her to be healed from the sickness that plagued her for twelve years. Below is the sermon outline that Jesus gave with the keys to receiving anything from God.

> 1. *SHE SAID. This woman heard how Jesus healed every sickness and disease, the lame, blind, and raised the dead. After she heard of Jesus, she believed what she heard and said so. What she said was her*

faith speaking. She said, "If I can touch his clothes, I know I shall be whole." Her confession built the road for her healing. Most translations say that she kept on saying continually. That word say in this verse in the Greek is the word "Lego," which means a systematic set discourse. She could have said, "It's been twelve long years, I might as well give up!" She could have laid down and died. But if you would have passed this woman, you would have heard her say over and over, "When I touch Jesus' clothes, I know I shall be made whole." **What you say will determine your victory or defeat.**

2. *SHE ACTED, SHE DID. Her faith moved her to action. She got up and began walking, pressing through the crowd. She could have said she was too weak to get out of her house, listening to her family telling her to stay in bed. Instead, she set in motion a process that got her off the sickbed and on the way to her miracle. Just like the people of God, in Numbers 21, who were*

being bitten by snakes looked at the brazen serpent and lived, the woman with the issue of blood took her eyes off herself and focused only on touching Jesus, the Healer.

3. SHE RECEIVED IT, AND SHE FELT in her body she was healed. The saying and doing preceded the feeling and healing. It enabled her to receive the healing power of Jesus. Her hand of faith reached out, laid hold on Jesus' clothes and Jesus felt that power go out of Him to heal her. Johnson translation says, "Jesus studied the faces in the crowd to see who had made contact with him."

4. SHE TOLD IT. When you testify about what God has done, you give glory to God and it keeps you in position for the power of God to continue to work. The same faith that makes you whole, will keep you whole. Jesus told her to go in peace and be made continually whole of the plague. Her faith took hold of the power of God.

These four steps of faith radically changed this woman's life. It was like Jesus had said to her, "Your next twelve years will not be like your last twelve years!"

"Anyone can be changed by faith, no matter how he may be fettered." -Smith Wigglesworth

You can also see these four steps in action in several places throughout the Bible. For instance, when David killed the giant, Goliath, he said, he did, he saw the giant fall, and he testified by cutting off the giant's head. The prodigal son said he would rise and go home. When he did, the father received and restored him, and the testimony was a party. When you rejoice, you are testifying that it is done, and the victory is won! You overcome by the blood of the Lamb and the word of your testimony.

REMEMBER THAT GOD LOVES YOU

There is a door of faith and expectation that opens when you realize how much God loves you and what He has done for you in redemption. His faith penetrates your heart and every trace of doubt melts away as you receive His love. Luke 12:32 says, "Fear not, little flock, for it is the Father's good pleasure to give you the kingdom." If He gave you Jesus, how much more will He freely give you all things? Draw near to the Father by the blood and spend time in His presence until you have full assurance of faith. It really is His pleasure to give you whatever you ask. Ask, and you shall receive, that your joy may be full!

The simplest
definition of faith
is to act like
the Bible is true.

5

MAKING JESUS MARVEL

CHAPTER FIVE

There are only two times in the Gospels where it says Jesus marveled. When you think about how long Jesus has been around and all He has seen, you can understand how it would take a lot to make Him marvel. We are talking about the Almighty God, the Creator of the ends of the earth. What made such an impression on Jesus that those around Him noticed how He marveled?

TWO KINDS OF UNBELIEF

The first time Jesus marveled was at unbelief. Jesus had gone into his hometown to preach. His family and friends were amazed at His teaching but refused to believe Him. They only saw Him naturally. That familiarity limited His power. As He said, a prophet is without honor in his own country. The scripture says in Mark 6:5-6, "And he could there do no mighty work, save that he laid his hands upon a few sick folk, and healed them. And he MARVELED because of their UNBELIEF. And he went round about the villages, teaching." It is simply astounding. He could do no mighty works in that place because of unbelief.

There are two kinds of unbelief. The first kind is ignorance — you just don't know. Here, we see that the cure for unbelief which comes from ignorance, is teaching. T.L. Osborn said, "Many of you are waiting until I quit teaching for you to get your healing. I am waiting for you to get your healing so I can quit teaching."[2] The cure for this kind of unbelief is the teaching of the Word of God. Romans 10:17 says, "Faith comes by hearing and hearing by the Word of God." Dad Hagin said, "Unbelief is the thief of God's best blessings." Unbelief is curable. If you can cure unbelief, you can cure anything.

Your faith cannot go beyond your knowledge of God's Word. Every breakthrough in faith comes from a breakthrough in revelation. Praying the prayers in Ephesians 1:17-23 and 3:14-21 will give you breakthroughs in revelation and move you to another level of faith.

The second kind of unbelief comes as a result of disobedience, stubbornness, and lack of persuasion to act on God's Word. It is because of this kind of unbelief the children of Israel did not enter the Promised Land (Hebrews 3:19 and Hebrews 4). The cure for this kind of unbelief is to be persuaded to obey and to act on God's Word. James 2:17 says, "Faith without works is dead." Faith must have corresponding action. "… but be ye doers of the Word, and not hearers only, deceiving your own selves," James 1:22. The simplest definition of faith is to act like the Bible is true. While looking at Mark 11:23, the Lord said it to me this way, ***"Faith moves God; faith moves mountains; but faith won't move anything until it moves you, and the first part of you your faith must move is your mouth."*** Speaking is the initial act of faith.

JESUS MARVELS AT GREAT FAITH

The second time we see that Jesus marveled was in Matthew 8 when the centurion came to get healing for his servant. Jesus offered to come and heal him, but the centurion wanted only to hear Him give the command of authority. "Speak the word only, and my servant shall be healed," Matthew 8:8. The centurion understood authority. If Jesus spoke the Word, it was just as good as a personal visitation from Jesus Himself. The centurion's faith brought Jesus to a standstill. This kind of faith was exactly what Jesus was looking for.

> *When Jesus heard it, he MARVELED, and said to them that followed, Verily I say unto you, I have not found so great faith, no, not in Israel. And Jesus said unto the centurion, Go thy way; and as thou hast believed, so be it done unto thee. And his servant was healed in the selfsame hour. -Matthew 8:10, 13*

YOU CAN SCHOOL YOURSELF INTO GREAT FAITH

God is still looking for great faith today. What has God spoken to you? The Word of God was written so that it could be spoken. I like what Lilian B. Yeomans said: ***"God has tied Himself irrevocably to human cooperation in the execution of Divine purposes. He has made man's faith a determining factor in the work of redemption."***[3] Remember that God's Word in your mouth is just as powerful as His Word in His mouth. The moment you act on God's Word, He makes Himself responsible for the results.

Your voice

is your address

in the realm

of the spirit.

Faith is voice-activated.

6

THE SPEECH
CENTER EXERCISES
DOMINION
CHAPTER SIX

In a recent study, a leading neurosurgeon discovered that the speech center of the brain exercises dominion over the entire central nervous system. He found that different parts of the body respond with stimuli to corresponding parts of the human brain. However, when the speech center is stimulated, the entire central nervous system responds. This means when someone says, "I am weak," the speech center sends out the message to the whole body to prepare to be weak. This must be the reason God said, "Let the weak say, I am strong," Joel 3:10.

BY YOUR WORDS

For in many things we offend all. If any man
offend not in word, the same is a perfect man,
and able also to bridle the whole body.
-James 3:2

Actually, James 3 makes it clear that the tongue controls not only the body, but the destiny and quality of our lives as well:

If you could find someone whose speech was
perfectly true, you'd have a perfect person, in
perfect control of life. A bit in the mouth of a
horse controls the whole horse. A small rudder
on a huge ship in the hands of a skilled captain
sets a course in the face of the strongest winds. A
word out of your mouth may seem of no account,
but it can accomplish nearly anything — or
destroy it! -James 3:2-5, Message

This study may seem to be a new discovery in medical science, but the Bible has been teaching this fact for thousands of years. Medical science is finally finding out that what the Bible has been saying has been true all along.

For he that will love life, and see good days, let him refrain his tongue from evil, and his lips that they speak no guile." -1 Peter 3:10

One of the first things a doctor does when examining you is to look at your tongue. Much the same, when you go to God with a problem, He says, "I see the problem. It is written all over your tongue."

The speech center is the dominion center for our lives. Our words will make us or break us. Our words determine the boundaries of our lives. Our words can limit us or loose us. God gave Adam dominion in the beginning through the power of the spoken word. That dominion is still true. The Lord Jesus, the Last Adam, said, "By thy words thou shalt be justified, and by thy words thou shalt be condemned," Matthew 12:37.

Jesus also gave us a revelation of how speaking by faith works in Mark 11:23 when He said, "Whosoever shall say...he shall have whatsoever he saith." Few people take this revelation as seriously as the Bible emphasizes.

GOD TOUCHES YOUR MOUTH
TO CHANGE YOUR WORLD

Anytime God wants to change our life, He touches our mouth. God changes lives through "mouth-to-mouth resuscitation." He puts His Words in our mouth to bring life, salvation, and healing.

When God wants to change a city or nation, He always touches someone's mouth. God touched Isaiah's mouth with a coal of fire and sent him to speak words that changed a nation. Those same words are still changing lives today — thousands of years later. God touched Jeremiah's mouth and not only changed his life, but an entire nation. The list of people God has used to change nations is long, but the most important thing is for God to touch your mouth and change your world through your words.

MAN IS A SPEAKING SPIRIT

And the Lord God formed man of the dust of the ground, and breathed into his nostrils the breath of life; and man became a living soul.
-Genesis 2:7

In Genesis 2:7, the phrase "man became a living soul," is better translated "a speaking spirit." God created man in His own image with the capacity to speak and communicate. The power of speech is a major distinguishing factor between the animal kingdom and man. Man was made a speaking spirit and given authority and dominion. Satan recognizes the power of spoken words and is constantly trying to get man to speak words that contaminate, defile and destroy. A constant war is going on for "air time." Satan wants to stop the spoken Word of God in your personal life, as well as in your city or nation.

YOUR VOICE IS YOUR TICKET OUT OF SATAN'S DOMINION

Say unto them, As truly as I live, saith the Lord, as ye have spoken in mine ears, so will I do to you. -Numbers 14:28

The story of the nation of Israel's failure to possess the Promised Land is clearly described in Numbers 13 and 14. Everyone in these two chapters got exactly what they said. There were twelve spies sent to spy out the land and bring back a report. Ten of the spies

came back and said, "We are not able," and they died
in the wilderness. But two of the spies, Joshua and
Caleb, won the war of words when they confidently
proclaimed, "We are well able to possess the land."

*Your voice is your address in the realm of the
spirit.* Your words custom design and specifically
shape your own future. Your speech center exercises
dominion in your life.

YOU HAVE BEEN FRAMED

*Through faith we understand that the worlds
were framed by the Word of God, so that things
which are seen were not made of things which
do appear. -Hebrews 11:3*

You often hear these words when working with
prison inmates, "I have been framed." However, the
person speaking them does not realize how true those
words really are. The truth is this: everyone has been
framed. Our words and the words of others have
framed our world.

Faith always consists of the spoken Word of God.
F.F. Bosworth said, "It is impossible to boldly claim by

faith a blessing that you are not sure God is offering."[4] You cannot boldly possess things you don't realize are available to you. If your confession is wrong, your thinking is wrong, and you will do without God's best blessings.

As we speak the Word of God, it tears down, roots out, builds, and plants our world (Jeremiah 1:4–12). God wants us to speak His Words and frame the picture He has for us. He has a custom plan for each of us in Christ Jesus.

> *For we are his workmanship, created in Christ*
> *Jesus unto good works, which God hath before*
> *ordained that we should walk in them.*
> *-Ephesians 2:10*

"LEGO" BIBLE BUILDING BLOCKS

Jesus said in Mark 11:23, "Whosoever shall *say*... shall believe those things which he *saith*...he shall have whatsoever he *saith*." Notice He said believe once and say, saith, saith three times. Dad Hagin explained the Lord instructed him that he would have to do three times more teaching on the speaking part of faith than on the believing part or people wouldn't get it. The speaking part of faith is vital. Faith is released or put into action by speaking. If you are silent, you lose by default.

In Mark 11:23, Jesus used three different Greek words to explain the speaking part of faith. The first "say" is the Greek word *epo*, which means command. It shows the authority of the believer. The second reference to speaking is the word "saith." This word in the Greek is *laleo*, which means to speak out, use your own voice, and be bold. The third reference to speaking is also the word "saith." However, this Greek word is *lego* which means a systematic set discourse.

At toy stores we see Lego sets that contain building blocks for children to construct according to the diagram or picture on the box. Jesus said, "I am giving you a set of Lego building blocks you can use to frame your world according to the picture and diagram I have given to you in the Word of God."

The Bible has given us a set of building blocks for salvation, healing, blessing, prosperity, and victory in life. Take the Word of God and build by putting His Word in your mouth and framing your future.

"Your success and usefulness in this world will be measured by your confession and your tenacity to hold fast to that confession." [5]

-F. F. Bosworth

In other words, do not just speak the confession, but be tenacious about it as well. God can be no bigger in you than you confess Him to be.

A spiritual law few people recognize is your situations and circumstances are not what determine your future. Your words and your confessions are what shape and determine who you are and what you will become.

God's Word didn't come
out of His pen, it came
out of His mouth.
It was spoken before it
was written, and it was
written so it could be spoken.

7

THE PERFECT LANGUAGE

CHAPTER SEVEN

I once read a book about a perfect language that existed in the beginning, which expressed the essence of all possible things. This must be the same creative language Adam spoke in the Garden of Eden. It is the language of dominion, of complete fellowship with God, a language of faith — it is the perfect language. This language was so powerful that even in man's fallen condition at the Tower of Babel, the Bible says anything they imagined to do was possible (Genesis 11:1-9). God had to confuse their languages to limit their ability and to prevent them from building the city and the tower.

It is this language of dominion that Jesus came to restore. It is the language of redemption and it contains the culture of Heaven. Now, if any man be "In Christ" he is a new creation, possessing a new kind of life. This new creation must learn a new language. The Bible contains this language that gives access into the thoughts and purposes of God. Learning a new language means you do not just speak it, but you understand it as well. Some have said you are not fluent in a language until you can think and even dream in that language.

There is a language every Christian must learn, the language of the cross. "For the preaching of the cross is to them that perish foolishness; but unto us which are saved it is the power of God," 1 Corinthians 1:18. My favorite translation calls it, "the language of redemption," (CEB). The "language of redemption" brings an understanding of what happened in the death, burial and resurrection of Christ. The same power that was in the events of the cross is in the message. This means that satan is just as afraid of the message as he is of the events of the death, burial and resurrection of Christ. This is a perfect language and a powerful language.

FAITH IN THE GOSPEL MESSAGE: THE WORD OF HIS POWER

God's Word did not come out of His pen, it came out of His mouth. Matthew 4:4 says, "It is written, man shall not live by bread alone, but by every word that proceedeth out of the mouth of God." It was spoken before it was written and it was written so it could be spoken. It is a spoken thing. "...Upholding all things by the word of his power," Hebrews 1:3. Paul said he was not ashamed of the Gospel of Christ, for it is the power of God to everyone who believes it (Romans 1:16,17).

FAITH IS FOR WHOSOEVER

Whosoever means: everybody won't, anybody can, and somebody will! The power of God is for WHOSOEVER believes and calls on the name of the Lord. "Whosoever shall say unto this mountain, be thou removed, and be thou cast into the sea; and shall not doubt in his heart, but shall believe that those things which he saith shall come to pass; he shall have whatsoever he saith," Mark 11:23. Whosoever shall have whatsoever!

FAITH'S CREATIVE WORDS

The door to the supernatural swings on two hinges: believing and speaking. All God's creation came into existence by speaking. Sound came before sight! God said, then He saw. Man is a speaking spirit, made in the image of God. We live by faith, which involves believing and speaking. "We having the same spirit of faith, according as it is written, I believed, and therefore have I spoken; we also believe, and therefore speak," 2 Corinthians 4:13.

As we looked at in Mark 11:23, there is an emphasis on the saying of the believer. Jesus commands the believer to *say* three different times. The third saith, translated *lego* in the Greek, means "a set discourse." In Mark 5, the woman who was healed when she touched Jesus' clothes had a set discourse. She kept speaking what she believed. "It shall come to pass" means you are on a journey. The moment she began to say, she was on the way; the exact words she continually said were coming to pass.

FAITH WORKS THROUGH THE CONTINUAL PRAISE IN YOUR MOUTH

Continual praise will bring continual victory! Our sacrifice of praise is to be in our mouth continually (Psalm 34:1). Hebrews 13:15 says it is the fruit of our lips giving thanks continually, or confessing to His Name that brings about supernatural victory. Out of the mouth of babes thou hast ordained praise to still the enemy (Psalm 8:2). When Paul and Silas were in jail, their praying and singing praises set everyone free (Acts 16:25,26).

FAITH'S SPIRITUAL LANGUAGE: SPEAKING WITH TONGUES

He that speaketh in an unknown tongue speaketh... unto God (1 Corinthians 14:2). God has given every Christian the means to strengthen themselves spiritually by speaking in tongues. "But ye, beloved, building up yourselves on your most holy faith, praying in the Holy Ghost," Jude 20. This kind of speaking will assist you in the worship of God, bring refreshing to your spirit-man, help you pray the perfect will of God, and speak mysteries untold. It is an unlimited language. "...be filled with the Spirit; speaking..." (Ephesians 5:18-19).

Let's take advantage of our unique ability to speak the perfect spiritual language of redemption, faith, and praise. This language is the expression of the kingdom of God and will release the power and the atmosphere of Heaven on Earth.

Your faith

will never rise above

your level of confession.

8

HOLD FAST TO YOUR CONFESSION

CHAPTER EIGHT

Seeing then that we have a great high priest,
that is passed into the Heavens, Jesus the Son
of God, let us hold fast our profession.
-Hebrews 4:14

There is a big difference between being an amateur and a professional. An amateur may play golf on the weekends, but a professional can make a living with it. The professional will even pay a coach to critique him to better his skills so he can win. You would never trust a heart surgeon to operate on you if he drove up pulling a trailer with lawn mowing equipment.

What if he said, "Yes, I do open heart surgeries, but I supplement my income by mowing lawns." You would definitely look for a more successful surgeon.

A true Christian does not just practice faith on the weekends, but lives it daily. It is his profession. In the Greek, the word for profession and the word for confession is the same, *homologia.*[6] It means "to say the same thing; to agree with; an acknowledgment or profession." It is more than just speaking. It is a lifestyle which affects every facet of life. As a Christian, your confession is your profession.

GET A GRIP ON YOUR LIP
AND DON'T LET IT SLIP

When I was in high school, our football team was undefeated. In preparation, there were times the coach would make the running back carry the ball all week in school so he could practice holding on to it. During the game, he might run the ball to the end zone, but he could not relax his grip until he crossed the goal line. The running back must become very conscious of the ball when facing the giants on the opposing team because he must have that ball in his hands in order to score.

You must realize the devil will do anything to make you fumble or to slap your confession out of you, but Hebrews 4:14 commands us to hold fast to it. The Message Bible says, "Let's not let it slip through our fingers." 1 Timothy 6:12 says, "Fight the good fight of faith, lay hold on eternal life, whereunto thou art also called, and hast professed a good profession before many witnesses." Your confession declares Jesus is Lord and is the key to winning the fight of faith. It notifies the devil you are off limits, for you are the property of God.

THE GREAT CONFESSION: JESUS IS LORD

That if thou shalt confess with thy mouth the Lord Jesus, and shalt believe in thine heart that God hath raised him from the dead, thou shalt be saved. For with the heart man believeth unto righteousness; and with the mouth confession is made unto salvation. -Romans 10:9, 10

A fundamental practice in your Christian faith is the initial and continual confession that Jesus Christ is Lord. He is Supreme Authority. The overriding emphasis is that He is Victor! When you declare that Jesus is Lord, you are saying more than you can comprehend. Jesus Christ not only got His name by inheritance, but by conquest.

Forasmuch then as the children are partakers of flesh and blood, he also himself likewise took part of the same; that through death he might destroy him that had the power of death, that is, the devil. -Hebrews 2:14

Wherefore God also hath highly exalted him, and given him a name which is above every name: That at the name of Jesus every knee should bow, of things in Heaven, and things in earth, and things under the earth; And that every tongue should confess that Jesus Christ is Lord, to the glory of God the Father.
-Philippians 2:9-11

I like to say it this way: ***When Jesus was raised from the dead, He stepped from the tomb as absolute master of death in all of its phases; hell and all of its hosts; of Satan and all of his works;***

of sin and all of its consequences. He was the first of a redeemed, restored, victorious humanity that would follow. He is the Firstborn from the dead; the first Man to enter the death experience and master it. Jesus is Lord.

RESTORATION, FELLOWSHIP, AND POSSESSION

Faith trembles in the darkness of broken fellowship. 1 John 1:9 is written to the Christian who still has a relationship with God, but has sinned and lost that fellowship he once enjoyed.

If we confess our sins, he is faithful and just to forgive us our sins, and to cleanse us from all unrighteousness. -1 John 1:9

This kind of confession is where we repent and turn from sin. There is cleansing in Jesus' blood and immediate restoration to fellowship with God. It is repentance, not penance!

Be careful of a dual confession, of saying one thing in church and another thing at home. God is merciful and will never change His mind about you, or the gifts and callings He has bestowed upon you. We need to come boldly to the throne of grace. Do not keep talking about where you missed it or how badly you have sinned, but confidently hold fast to your confession of faith in Christ. He is your righteousness and the High Priest of your profession (Hebrews 3:1).

Wherefore, holy brethren, partakers of the Heavenly calling, consider the Apostle and High Priest of our profession, Christ Jesus.
-Hebrews 3:1

For we do not have a High Priest Who is unable to understand and sympathize and have a shared feeling with our weaknesses and infirmities and liability to the assaults of temptation, but One Who has been tempted in every respect as we are, yet without sinning. Let us then fearlessly and confidently and boldly draw near to the throne of grace (the throne of God's unmerited favor to us sinners), that we may receive mercy [for our failures] and find grace to help in good time for every need [appropriate help and well-

timed help, coming just when we need it].

-Hebrews 4:14-16, Amplified

As your High Priest, Jesus has triumphed over all things. The moment you confess faith in Him, the enemy can no longer lord anything over you. Hold fast to your confession because it will defeat the devil and bring victory. God watches His Word to perform it. Charles Wesley wrote these powerful words in his hymn, "O For a Thousand Tongues to Sing:" *He breaks the power of canceled sin. He sets the prisoner free. His blood can make the foulest clean. His blood avails for me.*[7] Amen!

A CONTINUAL AND PUBLIC CONFESSION

By him therefore let us offer the sacrifice of praise to God continually, that is, the fruit of our lips giving thanks to his name.

-Hebrews 13:15

The word "thanks" here is the same Greek word meaning to confess and acknowledge.[8] Your faith lives and flourishes as your mouth is continually filled with praise. That praise is private, but must not stay that way. It is to be public as well. In fact, Jesus said, Whosoever therefore shall confess me before men, him will I confess also before my Father which is in Heaven (Matthew 10:32). Every time you speak of the Lordship of Christ to another person, Jesus will confess you before the Father. Your confession on the earth moves Heaven and brings the power and conviction of the Holy Spirit where you are.

> *Let us hold fast the profession of our faith without wavering; (for he is faithful that promised). -Hebrews 10:23*

> *Let's keep a firm grip on the promises that keep us going. He always keeps his word. Let's see how inventive we can be in encouraging love and helping out, not avoiding worshiping together as some do but spurring each other on, especially as we see the big Day approaching. -Message*

Jesus is coming soon, so hold fast to your confession, not just on the weekend or at church, but continually. Jesus is Victor!

FOUR AREAS A CHRISTIAN SHOULD INCLUDE IN DAILY CONFESSION:

1. *What God has done for us in the death, burial and resurrection of Christ.*

2. *Who we are now in Christ.*

3. *What Jesus is doing now for us in Heaven.*

4. *What God by the Word and the Holy Spirit can do in us now.*

THINGS TO REMEMBER:

1. *Confession builds the road over which faith carries its mighty cargo.*[9]

2. *A spiritual law few recognize is that our confessions rule us.*[10]

3. *Faith will never rise above the level of your confession.*[11]

4. *God can be no bigger in you than you confess Him to be.*[12]

5. *Many Christians are weak, though sincere, because they lack a bold confession of who they are in Christ.*[13]

6. *The confession of your lips that has grown out of faith in your heart will absolutely defeat the adversary in every combat.*[14]

7. *The Word will heal you if you will continually confess it.*[15]

8. *Nothing will establish and build your faith as quickly as confession.*[16]

9. *Your success and usefulness in this world is measured by your confession and the tenacity with which you hold fast to that confession.*[17]

God has ordained

strength to come out

of your mouth

to stop the enemy.

9

THE PRAISE CURE
CHAPTER NINE

I will bless the Lord at all times: his praise shall continually be in my mouth. -Psalm 34:1

When I was a teenager, I went to Tanzania where I stayed with missionaries Ralph and Shirley Hagemier for the summer. I remember going out into the bush to preach in churches, but one thing still stands out to me today. The African Christians lifted their voices to praise with all their heart and strength. I did the American style of praising for about thirty seconds and thought I was finished. But these believers would not stop. It was not until the pastor finally went to the pulpit and began to ring a bell that the worshipers quieted! He told me they had a problem. Their problem was they did not know when to stop praising God. I told him we had a similar problem in America, but it was the opposite, we had to play all kinds of music to get them started!

Praise is vocal. It can be both seen and heard by others. In Acts 16, Paul and Silas were bound, their hands and feet in stocks, but the authorities forgot to tape their mouths shut. I like to say, as long as you have your voice, there is no prison that can hold you!

Dr. Lilian B. Yeomans, in her book <u>Healing From Heaven</u>,[18] tells about a missionary to China who had ministered fearlessly to a sister missionary with smallpox. A very bad case of confluent smallpox broke out on her, and she did not know what to do. She asked the Lord for direction and He told her to sing and praise Him for His faithfulness to His Word. They isolated her and told her to lie quiet, but she insisted that if she did not praise God, the very stones would cry out. So she sang and sang and praised and praised. The doctor treating her feared for her life, as the case was serious and awful complications threatened. Yet she praised and praised and sang and sang.

The doctor was convinced she was delirious, but that he had so little help that he could not restrain her — and she sang and sang and praised and praised. They told her that if by any chance she recovered, she would be disfigured for life — and she sang and praised louder than ever. When they finally asked, "Why do you praise so much?" She answered, "Because I have so many pox on me. God showed me I must praise Him for each one separately." And she kept right at it.

The Lord had shown her a vision of two baskets, one containing her praising, which was half filled and the other her testing, which was completely filled. He told her that the praise basket must be filled in order to out balance the other, so she kept at it. Her songs and shouts were so Spirit-filled that they were contagious, and the Christian nurses could not resist joining in; they kept the place ringing. At last, the Lord showed her that the praise basket was full and overflowing. She saw the praise basket sink with the weight of her praises, and the testing basket rise in the air. In a moment, as it seemed, all the symptoms vanished, leaving no trace in the way of so much as a single scar.

Yes, ***the praise cure works every time.*** It is not unpleasant; rather it is delightful. The cost of it has been met, and it is available this moment to each of us. The last part of 1 Peter 1:8 tells us exactly how to begin, "Believing, ye rejoice with joy unspeakable and full of glory." Just believe what God says Jesus has done for you — body, soul, and spirit. When you think about it, talk about it, sing about it, shout about it, the praise cure has begun. You are not to take it once a year, but all the time.

PRAISE MOVES HEAVEN

In 2 Chronicles 20, when God's people began to sing and to say, "Praise the Lord; for his mercy endureth forever," the Lord sent ambushments against the enemies and the people of God were three days gathering the spoil! God has ordained strength to come out of our mouth to still the enemy (Psalm 8:2). Jesus used the word "praise" for strength in Matthew 21:16.

Abraham staggered not at the promises of God. I like to say, "You may not be an astronaut, but you can be a 'staggernot.'" Sometimes the promises of God seem so great that many stagger at the possibility they could belong to them. Romans 4:20,21 says, "He staggered not at the promise of God through unbelief; but was strong in faith, giving glory to God; And being fully persuaded that, what he had promised, he was able also to perform." Your praise will cause you to be fully persuaded. O magnify the Lord, let us exalt His name together!

The same power that was in the actual event of the death, burial, and resurrection of Christ is in the message of the Gospel.

10

THE POWER OF
THE GOSPEL
CHAPTER TEN

I was reading the book, <u>How Things Work</u>, learning how such things as washing machines and car engines work. I came across the chapter called "How Nuclear Energy Works." It caught my attention. I began to compare natural energy with supernatural power. Nuclear power plants provide 17% of the world's electricity, as well as power nuclear submarines and aircraft carriers. When a single atom splits, an incredible amount of energy is released. Uranium is the heaviest and the best example of a naturally radioactive element. The most commonly used isotope in creating nuclear power is a material called U-235.

When it undergoes fission, an immense amount of energy is produced. This process occurs quickly — in about one picoseconds, or one millionth of a second.

For fission to be effective the uranium sample must be enriched so it contains 2%-3% U-235. In a nuclear bomb, you want uranium to undergo fission as quickly as possible, releasing all the energy in an instant and creating a gigantic explosion. A pound of highly enriched uranium used to power a nuclear submarine or nuclear aircraft carrier is equal to about a million gallons of gasoline. When you consider the fact that a pound of uranium is smaller than a baseball and a million gallons of gasoline would fill a cube as tall as a five story building, you get an idea of the amount of energy available in just a little bit of enriched U-235![19]

THE PRAYER THAT ENRICHES FAITH

Just as uranium can be enriched, so can your faith. The first thing we need is knowledge of *Dunamis*, the God kind of power. What is this dunamis power? *It is inherent power; power for performing miracles; moral power and excellence of soul; the power and influence which belong to riches and wealth; power and resources arising from numbers; power consisting in or resting upon armies, forces, hosts.*[20]

This power is in the blood of Christ and it cleanses us from the very root of sin. This power is the same power that raised Jesus from the dead. Paul gives us a prayer we can pray in Ephesians. These are some of the words used to try to describe the great power that raised Jesus from the dead.

> *And what is the exceeding greatness of His power to usward who believe, according to the working of His mighty power which He wrought in Christ when he raised Him from the dead, and set Him at His own right hand in the Heavenly places. -Ephesians 1:19,20*

> *...the limitless scope (Translator's)...incredibly immense strength (Johnson)...great beyond measure (Laubach)...extraordinary power... it is the enormous overmastering supremacy (Cornish)...incredible outburst of his might (Centenary)...transcendently great (Wade)... super abounding greatness (Weust)*

Just think about the resurrection power used to raise Christ from the dead. It was the same identical power that made you a new creation when you confessed Jesus as Lord. It is activated when you believe and speak the language of faith in God. Romans 12:3 tells us God has dealt to every man a measure of this faith substance. It is like nuclear power, but much greater. It is energy to explode and stop the power of darkness and death, and bring light and life.

Just as there is an exact formula in the substance of U-235, there is an exact formula of faith as well. The mountain moving formula which activates this resurrection power is *believing with the heart* and *speaking with your mouth*. It only takes a mustard seed faith to move a mountain. It is the identical faith God has. Jesus commanded us to have this God-kind of faith in Mark 11:22.

This faith can be enriched by praying in the language of the Holy Spirit. One of the first times I experienced this to be true was on a trip to Africa, as a young man, to preach. I spent a whole day praying in tongues and really had no great feeling of power at the time. However, that night in the service, the power of God was present and many people were healed and set free. "But ye, beloved, building up yourselves on your most holy faith, praying in the Holy Ghost," Jude 20. "But you shall receive power after that the Holy Ghost is come upon you...," Acts 1:8. "Wait on the Lord, receive the power so you can run and not grow weary, walk and not faint" Isaiah 40:31.

PREACH THE GOSPEL: RELEASE THE POWER

There is power to heal the sick and change lives in the Gospel. Jesus came, preached the Gospel, cast out devils, healed the sick and raised the dead. He commanded His followers to do the same. After the day of Pentecost, Christians went everywhere preaching that Jesus died, was buried, and raised up by the power of God on the third day. Everywhere they went, there were confirming signs of the power of God following the preaching of the Good News.

In Acts 14, when Paul preached in Lystra, a crippled man heard the Gospel and it gave him faith to be healed. Paul shouted at him, saying stand up on your feet! And he leaped up and walked. Explosive energy called resurrection power was released as he believed the Gospel. The same power that is in the actual events of the death, burial, and resurrection of Christ is in the message of the Gospel. The devil is just as afraid of the message as he is of the events.

That power has not changed and is available for believers to walk in today. The Holy Spirit is still confirming the Good News with signs and wonders. We can all preach the Gospel and release the *dunamis* power of God to this generation!

On the day of Pentecost, the 120 people in the Upper Room were baptized into this power which gave them the ability to do the same works Jesus did with the same boldness in prayer and preaching as Jesus had. These 120 people were immersed into the identical power that raised Jesus from death. They all began to speak in languages they had not learned, telling of God's goodness. Peter was so transformed by the power of the Holy Spirit that he preached mightily, and three thousand people were saved! The results of this baptism of *dunamis* power shook the world.

THE GOSPEL IS THE POWER OF GOD

For I am not ashamed of the gospel of Christ:
for it is the power of God unto salvation, to every
one that believeth; to the Jew first, and also to
the Greek. For therein   is the righteousness of
God revealed from faith to faith: as it is written,
The just shall live by faith. -Romans 1:16, 17

The power of God is revealed in the Gospel — a spoken message, which releases great joy. It makes you glad. It is the language of redemption. It comes from the Greek word, *euangelion.*[21] This word, together with its rendering of "good tidings and glad tidings," occurs one hundred and eight times in the New Testament, none of which intimate anything less than "finished redemption" in Christ. The classic Greek meaning is *"Good news from the battlefield or a battlefield victory."*

Paul defined the word *gospel* as being the message of the death, the burial, and the resurrection of Christ. Much emphasis is given to the declaration and explanation of it, as the Gospel contains the power of God. When you preach it, the Holy Ghost will help you. Angels respond because they desire to look into it (1 Peter 1:12). This good news is not man-made, but was announced by angels to the shepherds. The shepherd's' responses were to rejoice with exceeding great joy.

> *Moreover, brethren, I declare unto you the gospel which I preached unto you... for I delivered unto you first of all that which I also received, how that Christ died for our sins according to*

> *the scriptures; and that he was buried, and*
> *that he rose again the third day according to*
> *the scriptures. -1 Corinthians 15:1,3,4*

Here we see the Gospel is the telling of the message of the death, burial, and resurrection of Jesus. The significance of the resurrection of Christ is determined by the nature of His death. When we understand what happened on the cross, that Jesus took our curse, sin, and death, then we understand that His resurrection is *our* resurrection, *our* life, *our* blessing and *our* victory. Everything God did in Christ, in His death, burial, and resurrection was for us and is set to the credit of our account.

The more Paul walked with the Lord, suffered persecution, preached in the regions beyond, and was caught up in the Spirit, the more he desired to know Christ. After pouring out his life for the church, going on his three missionary journeys and witnessing signs and wonders, the most significant experience of Paul's life was the revelation of the death, burial, and resurrection of Jesus Christ, and the revelation of his union with Christ. The deepest cry of his heart was to know Him, not to keep the Law, but to possess Christ's righteousness by faith.

[For my determined purpose is] that I may know Him [that I may progressively become more deeply and intimately acquainted with Him, perceiving and recognizing the wonders of His person more strongly and more clearly], and that I may in the same way come to know the power outflowing from His resurrection [which it exerts over believers], and that I may so share His sufferings as to be continually transformed [in spirit into His likeness even] to His death.

-Philippians 3:10, Amplified

It's not just enough

to know the "Word" of God,

you must also know

the "God" of the Word.

11

BEFORE HIM WHOM
HE BELIEVED
CHAPTER ELEVEN

These words stood out to me as I studied the steps
of the faith Abraham took in Romans 4:17-21. Today,
believers all over the world follow in Abraham's
footsteps to receive from God. God has not changed
and neither has the way faith works. Notice the phrase
"before Him whom he believed." The words "before
Him" are also translated "in His presence" or "in His
sight." Abraham's faith was loaded with the presence
of God. He was God-conscious. I like to say that some
people are self-conscious, some are people-conscious,
some are devil-conscious, some are time-conscious,

and some are unconscious! But to win the fight of faith we must be God-conscious.

Abraham got up early in the morning to the place where he stood before the Lord.
-*Genesis 19:27*

NO LONG DISTANCE FAITH

Abraham had a habit of praying and standing before the Lord. He did not just have the promises of God, he also had the presence of God. He stood "before Him whom he believed." Abraham knew how to fellowship with God and practiced standing in the presence of God. He did not just know the "Word of God", he knew the "God of the Word." Abraham was a friend of God. He communed with God.

Sometimes it seems that believers try to win the faith fight without getting before God. They quote scriptures, but do not seem to know how to access the presence of God. They try to believe without spending time with Him. Some believers try to believe at a distance, but there is no such thing as long distance faith. We must draw near…close to the heart of God and believe in His presence (Hebrews 10:19-23).

Let us not stand at a distance as if God were
inaccessible; but, on the contrary, let us draw
near with a sincere and affectionate heart,
in the full assurance of faith, supported by
such considerations as these, which may well
embolden us…to make our approach unto Him
in the most cheerful expectation of His blessing.
-Hebrews 10:22, Doddridge

Let us as members of His family, exercise our
right of access and press closer and closer to the
Father…. -Hebrews 10:22, Lovett

In Christ, God has chosen us to stand before Him. We are standing in His presence, holy and without blame, because of His love for us. He is our Father and we are His children. God's plan has always been for us to live in His presence. Through faith in the blood of Jesus, we are brought before Him. We are granted access into the closest fellowship with the Father God because of Jesus. Now our faith is loaded with His presence, promise, and power.

According as He hath chosen us in him before the foundation of the world, that we should be holy and without blame before him in love.
-Ephesians 1:4

Christ brought us into the very presence of God and you are standing there before Him with nothing left against you....
-Colossians 1:22, The Living Bible

ACCESS GRANTED

For through Him we both have access by one Spirit unto the Father. -Ephesians 2:18

In whom we have boldness and access with confidence by the faith of Him.
-Ephesians 3:12

By whom also we have access by faith into this grace wherein we stand, and rejoice in hope of the glory of God. -Romans 5:2

These three verses speak of access, a term meaning admission into the presence of royalty. In Christ, we have not only been granted access, but have been granted an audience with the King. We may bring others before Him so they too can be changed. Before Him there is forgiveness of sins and healing for your body. In Luke 5:18, four men brought their paralyzed friend through the roof of the house where Jesus was and placed him before Him. The man went home forgiven, healed, and glorifying God.

David knew how to access the presence of God and he rejoiced before the Lord as the glory of God returned to the city of David. He actually brought the presence of God to a whole nation. David remembered how God anointed and chose him, and he danced before Him.

Our faith in Jesus literally brings us before God. We are the believers and God is the Performer. He will bring it to pass. Let us exercise our right of access and come before Him whom we believe. Together, we will experience great results as our faith in God grows stronger.

By faith we are
saying and seeing
what God has done
for us in Christ.

12

WHAT ARE YOU LOOKING AT?

CHAPTER TWELVE

How would you feel if the pilot on your next flight came on the intercom and said, "Today folks, I am not going to look at any of my instruments or listen to the air traffic controller. I am going to fly by my feelings. I think I can land us at our destination." You would want to get off that flight immediately! Did you know that without being instrument-rated, a pilot can only fly for 90 seconds without visual reference? That means when he gets into fog or clouds he'll become disoriented. He may feel like he is going the right direction when he is actually totally off course. You need a pilot who is instrument-rated for a safe flight. To be instrument-rated means you focus on your instruments rather than what you feel or perceive naturally.

A good pilot trusts his instruments to give him the true status of his altitude, position, airspeed, etc. This is how a Christian is to live life. We are to live by faith — by looking into the Word of God and fixing our eyes on Jesus. As believers, we are not trusting our feelings, but following the guidance of the Spirit of God.

YOU CAN BELIEVE WHEN YOU LOOK

Numbers 21 tells the story of how Moses prayed for the people who, because of their murmuring and complaining, were bitten by poisonous snakes. The Lord instructed him to make a "serpent of bronze and set it on a pole. If a poisonous snake had bitten any man, when he looked to the serpent of bronze [attentively, expectantly, with a steady and absorbing gaze], he lived." (verses 8, 9) Can you imagine the focus it required to keep a steady gaze on that brazen serpent while surrounded by the poisonous vipers biting at not only them, but also those around them? When they fixed their gaze on that serpent of bronze, they were healed and they lived. This was a prophetic picture of Jesus and how He became a curse for us on the cross. When Moses held up the serpent on the pole, it represented our sickness, our curse, our sin, our guilt, and our shame. As we look at the cross, we can see that we were crucified with Christ.

The words "to lift up" are very significant in the Greek.

> *The verb to lift up is "hupsoun." The strange thing is that it is used of Jesus in two senses. It is used of his being lifted up upon the Cross; and it is used of His being lifted up into glory at the time of his ascension into Heaven. It is used of the Cross in John 8:28; 12:32. It is used of Jesus' ascension into glory in Acts 2:33; 5:31; Philippians 2:9. There was a double lifting up in Jesus' life — the lifting on the Cross and the lifting into glory. And the two are inextricably connected. The one could not happen without the other.[22] -William Barclay*

Believing in what God did for us on the cross brings that "lifting power" to our individual lives. Jesus used the word "believe" when speaking about focusing on the cross. When we look at what Jesus did for us on the cross with an attentive, expectant, steady, and absorbing gaze, He calls that *"believing."* The power in His redemptive work and in the written Word is released into our hearts to give life, healing, and blessing. Believing means that you see with the eyes of your heart. By meditating on redemption you can absorb the power in it. You can receive the promises of God and all that the blood of Jesus has done for you in the death, burial, and resurrection of Christ Jesus. There is life when we look at the Cross!

JESUS WILL SAVE YOU
WHEN YOU LOOK

Remember the classic story about Jesus walking on the water, and how Peter got out of the boat to walk to Him? The Amplified Bible says that "when he perceived and felt the strong wind, he was frightened, and as he began to sink, he cried out, Lord, save me!" Instantly, Jesus reached out His hand and caught him. Holding him, Jesus said to him, "O you of little faith, why did you doubt?" Matthew 14:30, 31. The Living Bible says when he looked around at the high waves, he was terrified. Here again, we can see the direct effect your vision and focus have on your faith. A steadfast gaze on Jesus will remove all doubt and fear. There is saving power when you look at Jesus!

THERE IS POWER TO CHANGE AS YOU LOOK

What can be done when it seems as though you will never be able to change or it is impossible to be free from old attitudes and lifestyles? Consider this question: What are you looking at? The Word of God is compared to a mirror that you keep looking into until you change. This is the wisdom you are looking for.

For if any be a hearer of the word, and not a doer, he is like unto a man beholding his natural face in a glass: For he beholdeth himself, and goeth his way, and straightway forgetteth what manner of man he was. Be whoso looketh into the perfect law of liberty, and continueth therein, he being not a forgetful hearer, but a doer of the work, this man shall be blessed in his deed. -James 1:23-25

*But we all, with open face beholding as in a
glass the glory of the Lord, are changed into the
same image from glory to glory, even as by the
Spirit of the Lord. -2 Corinthians 3:18*

There is a supernatural transformation that occurs
when you keep your gaze fixed upon the Word, find
scriptures that paint a picture of the answer, let the
Holy Spirit reveal the face of Christ, and stamp it into
your heart. Receive God's blessing and transformation
as you look at His Word.

RECEIVE YOUR HEALING
WHEN YOU LOOK

*My son, attend to my words; incline thine ear
unto my sayings. Let them not depart from
thine eyes; keep them in the midst of thine heart.
For they are life unto those that find them, and
health to all their flesh. Keep thy heart with
all diligence; for out of it are the issues of life.
-Proverbs 4:20-23*

Seeing and hearing the Word of God is the door
you open for the power in that Word to come into

you. The power of God will displace sickness in your body and replace it with health in your spirit, soul, and body. Faith in God will grow automatically as you focus on the healing found in Him. You will find yourself believing for the impossible.

Pastor Yonggi Cho, pastor of the largest full gospel church in the world, shared his healing testimony in which he confessed out loud one thousand times, "By Jesus' stripes I am healed."[23] He received his healing as he focused his attention on that scripture. By speaking it, he absorbed its power into his spirit, soul, and body. Speak the Word like you would take medicine: with diligence and regularity. Miracles and healing will take place when you look.

THIS IS NO TIME FOR ATTENTION DEFICIT DISORDER

What is the Holy Spirit saying to the Church in these end times? What should we be doing when there are financial storms, vipers of fear, disease, and troubled times surrounding us? What are you looking at? This is no time for spiritual attention deficit disorder! Instead, focus on these powerful words from the Apostle Paul:

While we look not at the things which are seen, but at the things which are not seen: for the things which are seen are temporal; but the things which are not seen are eternal.

-2 Corinthians 4:18

In Christ, you can see invisible and eternal things. Hebrews 12:1,2 gives us our instructions for finishing this race with joy. First of all, realize that you are not alone, but rather, you have a mighty host in Heaven cheering you on. Next, remove every weight and sin hanging on you and keep running with your eyes fixed on Jesus. The Amplified Bible says, "Looking away from all that will distract, to Jesus, Who is the Leader and Source of our faith…." Forget those things you left behind. They are only distractions to trip you up. Keep an attentive, expectant, steady and absorbing gaze on Jesus, the Author and Finisher of your faith. There is certain victory when you look at Jesus!

Let us believe the Word of God and see ourselves crucified with Christ. Then we can see the believer's identification with Christ, the greatest revelation in the New Testament. Believing is seeing yourself in Christ, in His death and triumphant resurrection, with the eyes of your heart. Let your faith take hold of this truth: if you were crucified with Christ, you were also raised and lifted up with Him. From that perspective, your eyes behold His majesty and glory as you reach your destination and see Him face to face. Let us finish our course with joy!

If you will get addicted

to giving,

God will support

your habit.

13

WASABI MOMENTS: GOD IS WORKING ON MY BRAIN

CHAPTER THIRTEEN

For the weapons of our warfare are not carnal but mighty in God for pulling down strongholds, casting down arguments and every high thing that exalts itself against the knowledge of God, bringing every thought into captivity to the obedience of Christ. -2 Corinthians 10:4,5

The first experience I had eating sushi was unforgettable! I learned you could dip your roll into a mixture of soy sauce, and something called wasabi, and pop it into your mouth with one big bite. I was warned that all I needed was a little dab of this wasabi, because it is powerfully hot. But I'm a real man and really did not think it would affect me. So I added a heaping spoon to my sauce and proceeded to dip my sushi in it. I popped it into my mouth and waited a few seconds. Suddenly it felt like my entire brain was on fire.

I had an experience with wasabi that day that I liken to the effect of God's Word on your brain. When you get one of God's thoughts in your mind, it will explode old ways of thinking — pull down religious, carnal ways of thinking — and renew your mind with the mind of Christ. I call that a "wasabi experience!" We must be transformed by the renewing of our minds so we can experience the perfect will of God in every area of our lives. This involves exchanging our "lack thinking" for God's thinking.

TAPPING INTO GOD'S RESERVOIR OF ABUNDANCE

It seems there is an invisible reservoir of abundance that can be tapped by obeying certain spiritual laws.[24] *-Norman Vincent Peale*

When I was just a young man, I decided I did not want to be a broke preacher, a victim of my circumstances, or the pity of others. I began to study and practice the Biblical principles my father taught me on tithing and giving. I am grateful they modeled this lifestyle and taught me how to tap into a lifetime reservoir of abundance. I learned first-hand the blessings, reward, and favor that comes to whomever decides to make giving a lifestyle, not just an occasional event.

My dad and mom taught me to tithe the first ten percent of whatever money came into my hands. My dad said I could either tithe on what I made or I could tithe on what I wanted to make. That is when I began to give over and above my tithe, eventually tripling my tithe. My dad practiced giving generously throughout his life, giving fifty percent of his income to the church, missions, and other ministries that had blessed him. I was following his father's example.

My grandfather Hankins was saved, filled with the Holy Ghost, and went on to pioneer churches in Texas during the depression days. Once, when a missionary preached in their church, Pappaw Hankins gave that minister all the money he was saving for a much needed car. All the family was rather upset that the car fund was gone. Not long after, they were given a practically new car, much better than what they would have purchased. That experience taught my father the important lesson that it is more blessed to give than to receive. Proverbs 11:24, 25 is really true.

> *There is that scattereth, and yet increaseth; and there is that withholdeth more than is meet, but it tendeth to poverty. The liberal soul shall be made fat: and he that watereth shall be watered also himself. Proverbs 11:24,25*

> *One gives away, and he still grows the richer...*
> *-Moffat*

> *It is possible to give away and become richer! It is possible to hold on too tightly and lose everything. Yes, the liberal man shall be rich! By watering others, he waters himself.*
> *-Living Bible*

NOT VALID IF DETACHED

My dad learned that you could enter into partnership with the Father God. That is exactly what the Philippian church did. A partner receives a percentage of the increase of the business. ***When we tithe and give offerings over and above, we become business partners with God. It is to His advantage when you prosper!*** It is how His Kingdom is increased. However, some try to withdraw money from their bank account when they have never made a deposit.

I watched one day as a man tried over and over to withdraw money from a cash machine when he obviously did not have anything in his account. He finally threw his receipts on the ground and stomped off in frustration. I laughed to myself as I thought how it is the same with many Christians. There has to be a deposit made in order to make a withdrawal. Christians often quote Philippians 4:19 with no results because they have never made an investment of tithing and giving in their Heavenly bank account. I like to say, "If you will get addicted to giving, God will support your habit."

My friends at Philippi, you remember what it was like when I started preaching the good news in Macedonia. After I left there, you were the only church that became my PARTNER by giving blessings and by receiving them in return. Even when I was in Thessalonica, you helped me more than once. I am not trying to get something from you, but I want you to receive the blessings that come from giving. I have been paid back everything, and with interest. I am completely satisfied with the gifts that you had Epaphroditus bring me. They are like a sweet-smelling offering or like the right kind of sacrifice that pleases God. I pray that God will take care of all your needs with the wonderful blessings that come from Christ Jesus!

Philippians 4:15-19, CEV

In these scriptures, Paul told the Philippians how this debit and credit account worked for them. Because of their giving, they were entering into partnership with God. God could now supply all of their needs. P.C. Nelson, a Pentecostal theologian fluent in thirty two languages, taught that this passage was like a coupon, reading, "NOT VALID IF DETACHED."[25] Only when a believer gives as verse 16 says, "they gave once and again," can they claim verse 19, "My God shall supply all your need, according to His riches in glory by Christ Jesus."

DON'T TALK LACK

Dad Hagin said, "Never talk lack if you want God's blessing in your life!" Always say the money will come and the Lord is my shepherd. If we complain and talk lack, we are accusing God of child abuse. Always say that my Father takes care of me in grand style. God wants to bless you so much that He can use you are advertisement of how good He treats His children.

TAP INTO THIS GRACE

The Apostle Paul understood the religious duties of tithing and giving, but his revelation of the redemptive work changed it from just a duty to a partnership with God in His kingdom business. He understood how Jesus identified with man's extreme poverty, so that we could share Christ's divine life and prosperity. On the cross, He redeemed us from the curse of the law so that the blessing of Abraham could come on us making us truly rich.

For you see the grace of our Lord Jesus Christ,
how though he had wealth, he became poor on
you're account, so that through his need you
might have wealth.

-2 Corinthians 8:9, Bible in Basic English

...enriched, (abundantly supplied). -Amplified

...gain riches through His poverty. -Wood

2 Corinthians 8 and 9 are a picture of how we can enjoy Christ's redemptive work financially. Truly, it is more blessed to give than to receive. When the early church began to follow the example of Jesus, they found this reservoir that took them from great poverty to a great overflow. Paul left Titus in Corinth to make sure they continued in the grace of giving and carried out their commitment to finish the giving they had begun.

Therefore, as ye abound in every thing, in
faith, and utterance, and knowledge, and in all
diligence, and in your love to us, see that ye
abound in this grace also. -2 Corinthians 8:7

*Since you excel in so many ways — in your
faith, your gifted speakers, your knowledge,
your enthusiasm, and your love from us - I
want you to excel also in this gracious act of
giving. -New Living Bible*

In this scripture, Paul is telling us to see that we excel in this grace of giving. In other words, this is not something that happens automatically but we have to "see to it" that we excel in this area. By faith we access the grace of God in giving and receiving.

If grace is amazing in every other area of life, then it should also be amazing in the area of our finances and the blessing of the Lord. God wants His grace — His favor, His ability, His financial resources — to be so notable that one day you will drive up to your house and say, "Amazing Grace!" We access this grace by faith. By the grace of God, you are able to give more than you have ever given and still have more than you have ever had (2 Corinthians 9:6-10).

God is calling the church to rise up and to tap into His abundant grace. This reservoir of abundance can be tapped by obeying these four spiritual laws: The Law of Faith; The Law of Sowing and Reaping;

The Law of Love; and The Law of the Spirit of Life in Christ Jesus. These laws work together, causing us, the body of Christ, to release His authority, do His works, and be supplied with finances and favor to do His will in this time.

The Word will work

for you when you

get thrilled with it.

- Kenneth E. Hagin

14

MEDITATION...
HOW TO TAP INTO
HEAVEN'S SUPPLY
CHAPTER FOURTEEN

I like what Norman Vincent Peale said: "It's almost as if there were an invisible reservoir of abundance that can be tapped by obeying certain spiritual laws."[26] In difficult times people search out resources to sustain themselves. Those who put their trust in God and learn to tap into His supply will not lack and will even flourish. There is an art of meditation upon God's Word, which draws out His wisdom and His supernatural power to produce amazing results. Meditation is often overlooked and even skipped as we go through the daily affairs of life. It is important to study how to meditate as well as what to meditate on in order to see the results of Christian meditation.

But his delight is in the law of the Lord; and in His law doth he meditate day and night; and He shall be like a tree that's planted by the rivers of water, that bringeth forth his fruit in his season; his leaf also shall not wither and whatsoever he doeth shall prosper.
-Psalm 1:2,3

You thrill to God's Word, you chew on Scripture day and night. You're a tree replanted in Eden, bearing fresh fruit every month, never dropping a leaf, always in blossom. -Message

Most blessed is the man who believes in, trusts in, and relies on the Lord, and whose hope and confidence the Lord is. For he shall be like a tree planted by the waters that spreads out its roots by the river; and it shall not see and fear when heat comes; but its leaf shall be green, It shall not be anxious and full of care in the year of drought, nor shall it cease yielding fruit.
-Jeremiah 17:7,8, Amplified

He is like a tree planted along the riverbank,
with its roots reaching deep into the water — a
tree not bothered by the heat nor worried by long
months of drought. Its leaves stay green...
-Taylor

Most blessed is the man who trusts me, God,
the woman who sticks with God. They're like
trees replanted in Eden, putting down roots near
the rivers. Never a worry through the hottest
of summers, never dropping a leaf, serene and
calm through droughts, bearing fresh fruit every
season. -Message

He is like a tree by the water side that thrusts
its roots to the stream: when the heat comes it
feels no alarm, its foliage stays green; it has no
worries in the year of drought, and never ceases
to bear fruit. -Jerusalem

In 1 Timothy 4:15, Paul said to "meditate upon these things; give thyself wholly to them, that thy profiting may appear to all." When a tree is well watered, it is evident to all. The fruit is flourishing and the leaves are green. In the same way, those around you see the results of the Word working in your life. The fruit of blessing, health, and peace is very tangible.

HOW TO MEDITATE

The dictionary defines the word "meditate" as this: *to talk with yourself, mutter, cogitate; it is an inward and outward conversation; it means to study, chew over, think over, ponder, excogitate, muse, reflect, mull over, speculate.*[27] The word "cogitate"[28] means to think deeply, think out, think up, dream up, and to hatch. Excogitate is to invent; create mentally. Christian meditation is NOT sitting on the floor with your legs crossed, humming to yourself, and emptying your mind. Meditation is a relationship with the Word of God.

If you know how to worry or if you have been offended, you know how to meditate. When you are worried or offended, you constantly think about what could happen, what is happening, and speculate about the results of what did happen. This constant musing affects your body and emotions. The Bible originated in the East where the culture is given to meditation. Because of this, it has much to say about this exercise. Philippians 4:6,7 tells us not to worry about anything, but to turn those worries into requests followed by thanksgiving. God promises to surround your heart with His peace. According to verse 8, our part is to do something with our thoughts. We are to meditate, or think, about things that are true, honest, just, pure, lovely, of good report, virtuous, and begin praising instead of worrying.

> *According as His divine power has given unto us all things that pertain to life and godliness, through the knowledge of him that hath called us to glory and virtue: whereby are given unto us exceeding great and precious promises; that by these ye might be partakers of the divine nature, having escaped the corruption that is in the world through lust. -2 Peter 1:3,4*

As Christians, we do not have to participate in the corruption around us. There is an escape. Because of the new birth, you are a partaker of God's divine nature and have in you everything you need to overcome in life. Through meditation, the Word becomes engrafted in you and is able to save or restore your soul, which is your mind, will and emotions (James 1:21). When you are speaking the Word of God — pondering, muttering, turning it over, digesting, and dreaming about all of God's promises — you begin to draw up divine power in the same way a tree draws water out of the soil in which it is planted.

WHO ARE YOU WEARING

While watching the Academy Awards on television, the announcers began interviewing the actresses and discussing the beautiful designer gowns the ladies were wearing. I noticed the announcers asked the ladies WHO they were wearing. They were asking for the name of the dress' designer. Was it Versace, Oscar de la Renta, or maybe Vera Wang? Like those actresses, we must put on, or clothe ourselves with the garments of praise and robes of righteousness.

When a Christian meditates on who they are in Christ and allows the Holy Spirit to clothe them with power from Heaven, they are putting on, or wearing Christ. In Ephesians 4:23,24, Paul says, "be renewed in the spirit of your mind...put on the new man, which is created in righteousness and true holiness." In the same fashion, Paul says in Romans 13:14, "put ye on the Lord Jesus Christ, and make not provision for the flesh, to fulfill the lusts thereof." You should not be wearing your old identity. God has designed new clothes for you to put on. Put on the consciousness of your redemption and who you are in Christ. As you do so, people around you will be able to see Jesus' love, joy, peace, ability, and wisdom reflected in and on you. You will bring glory to Him and people will ask, "Who are you wearing?"

FEAST ON THE WORD

Your words were found and I did eat them and they were to me the joy and rejoicing of my heart. - Jeremiah 15:16

When your words showed up, I ate them - swallowed them whole. What a feast!
-Message

When your words came, I devoured them.
-Jerusalem

Your words are what sustained me, they are food to my soul. -Taylor

My mother was the slowest eater I knew. We would start our meal together and two hours later she would still be chewing. I would tell her to take the rest of her dinner home because I had things to do. She would proceed to tell me the benefits of eating slowly.

Doctors say you should chew your food 32 times before swallowing. Digestion begins in your mouth, where the food is broken down before you swallow. God's Word is faith food and is meant to be eaten. "Man shall not live by bread alone, but by every word that proceedeth out of the mouth of God," Matthew 4:4. Faith comes by hearing and hearing by the Word of God. The Word must be digested for faith to come. When you meditate, the Word gets in your eyes, your ears, your mouth, and your heart. It permeates all of your body.

In Mark 4, Jesus taught the importance of hearing the Word by comparing it to seed. After planting the seed, the most important thing for the growth of any plant is for the roots to travel deep within the soil, causing growth and eventually fruit to come forth. Wherever you have a need in your life, begin to gather seeds of the Word, so you can plant them in your heart and grow that crop of healing, peace, finances, your family's salvation, etc.

1 Corinthians 3:6 says, "I have planted, Apollos watered; but God gave the increase." The planting occurs when you first hear the Word, but you cannot stop there. It must be watered by repetition. Some reject the watering process. As a result, they get no results from the Word they hear. If there is no increase, check out your watering or your meditation of the Word. Proverbs 4:20-22 instructs us to keep the Word in our mouth, before our eyes, and in our heart. When we do this, health is the result. Take it just like you would take medicine. He wants you to be well because He sent His Word to heal you (Psalm 107:20)!

DELIGHT IN THE LAW OF THE LORD

David said his delight was in the Law of the Lord. What are those laws? Those laws are His Word. They are the Law of Faith (Romans 3:27); the Law of Love (1 Corinthians 13); the Law of the Spirit of Life (Romans 8:2); the Law of Sowing and Reaping (2 Corinthians 9:6-11). Every Christian is personally responsible for tapping into the power of God in these areas in order to live above the corruption in the world. As we see in Psalm 119, the longest chapter in the Bible, David's love for God's Word overflows, and he mentions meditation seven times. Singing psalms like David did is a form of meditation.

> *I will sing unto the Lord as long as I live: I will*
> *sing praise to my God while I have my being.*
> *My meditation of him shall be sweet: I will be*
> *glad in the Lord, -Psalm 104:33,34*

GOD IS CLOSER THAN YOU THINK

There are warning signs on most rear-view mirrors that read, "the objects in the mirror are much closer than they appear." God is closer to you than you realize and when you acknowledge Him, He will respond to you. When Paul was in Athens, he addressed the philosophers on Mars' Hill who had an altar to the Unknown God. He told them about the God who made the Heaven and earth and how that if they would seek Him they would find Him. "...He be not far from every one of us: For in him we live, and move, and have our being...For we are also His offspring," Acts 17:27,28. God is not far from you and when you call on Jesus, when you acknowledge Him and His Word, you will tap into His Presence.

As you meditate on Hebrews 10:19-22, the Holy Spirit will paint a vivid picture of how, through the blood of Jesus, you have access with boldness into His throne room. God's Word will begin to flood your consciousness. You will tap into that great reservoir of abundance, love, and unlimited grace. You will have the mind of Christ. You will enter the realm where all things are possible.

Dad Hagin said it this way, "The Word will work for you when you get thrilled with it." It will walk off the page and into your heart, living and abiding in you, guiding you into good success every step of the way, every night and day. Fall in love with it! Eat it! Delight in it! Speak it! Sing it! Shout it!

The Spirit of Faith

will take the

victim out of your voice

and put victory

in your voice.

15

THE SPIRIT OF FAITH IS NOT FRAGILE

CHAPTER FIFTEEN

There is a popular old song, recorded by Patsy Cline, that used to come on the radio. Her rich voice sang a sad tune about how her lover left her and she just "fell to pieces." It's amazing to think one person could make you fall to pieces! Having heard this song on a TV advertisement, I started humming the catchy tune around my house. In the middle of my humming, the Holy Spirit stopped me and said, "Do not sing those words!" He reminded me that I am in Christ, and even in the middle of the worst circumstances I can say, "I DO NOT fall to pieces!" Jesus will take the victim out of your voice and replace it with a voice of faith. The Spirit of faith will put victory in your voice.

But we have this treasure in earthen vessels, that the excellency of the power may be of God, and not of us. We are troubled on every side, yet not distressed; we are perplexed, but not in despair; Persecuted, but not forsaken; cast down, but not destroyed; We having the same spirit of faith, according as it is written, I believed, and therefore have I spoken; we also believe, and therefore speak. -2 Corinthians 4:7-9, 13, 14

Paul had many reasons to fall to pieces, but instead, he thanked God for always causing him to triumph, even in the worst of circumstances. Paul's faith was not fragile. He was perplexed but not in despair. Have you experienced embarrassment, anxiety or times that left you puzzled at how you got into your very complicated situation? I don't have all the answers, but I know the One who does. I like Barclay's translation which says, "We are knocked down, but never knocked out."

In 2 Corinthians 11:24-27, we are given Paul's testimony. He was beaten with thirty nine stripes five times and with rods three times. He was stoned with rocks, in three shipwrecks, and spent a night and day in the deep water. He also listed being in perils by robbers, countrymen, heathens, and false brethren, in both the city and the wilderness. He was weary and in pain. He suffered hunger and thirst, and knew what it was to be cold and naked. His labors were more abundant, his stripes above measure, his imprisonments frequent, and threats of death often.

When standing on the ship on the third day of a fourteen day storm, he told the passengers and crew to cheer up because he believed God, and all would be safe. Paul even had forty enemies who refused to eat until they killed him. I have had people angry at me, but all of them ate. Paul did not fall to pieces. He had the same spirit of faith the psalmist David spoke about in Psalm 116:10 when he himself was greatly afflicted. After David's baby died, he did not fall to pieces, but rather he got up, changed his clothes, went to the temple, and worshiped. God not only restored David, but also gave him a son named Solomon who became the wisest and the richest king in history.

TAKE HOLD OF
GOD'S FAITHFULNESS AND ABILITY

My dad gave me some good advice about where to put my faith. He told me, "There is a God and I'm not Him!" He was teaching me to put my faith in

God rather than in people. Jesus said to have faith in God or to take hold of His faithfulness. Trust in God's ability. What is He able to do?

1. *God is able to keep you from falling and to present you faultless (Jude 24).*

2. *God is able to assist or relieve you when you cry to Him in testing (Hebrews 2:18).*

3. *God is able to deliver you from the fiery furnace of persecution (Daniel 3:17).*

4. *God is able to perform what He promised (Romans 4:21).*

5. *God is able to make all grace abound unto givers (2 Corinthians 9:8).*

6. *God is able to do exceeding abundantly above all you can ask or think (Ephesians 3:20).*

Paul said, "I know in whom I have believed." Job said, "I know my redeemer lives." When surrounded by uncertainty, nail down what you do know. Then, what you do not know will be unable to shake your faith.

OPENING THE DOOR
TO THE SUPERNATURAL

The door to the supernatural swings on two hinges: believing and speaking. You are the believer and God is the performer. When Trina had a brain tumor, I had to get a grip on my faith. It was not my job to do the supernatural, but to simply arrange a meeting between the "mountain" and God — to open the door to the supernatural. I commanded that tumor to dry up and to be removed. I simply opened the door and said, "Mr. Tumor, meet Jehovah!" At that point, Jehovah Rapha, the Healer, dissolved that tumor.

When a problem comes knocking on your door, open the door and introduce it to God. Then, step back and watch God do a miracle. Open the door to God's ability! When people ask you how you are feeling when you are going through the greatest trial of your faith, you simply say to them, "I'm feeling the same way Jesus was feeling when He overcame this feeling! I have faith in God. I am not fragile and I DO NOT FALL TO PIECES!"

Jesus has the
divine antibody in His blood
that overcomes sin and
all the curse sin brings.

16

FAITH IN HIS BLOOD

CHAPTER SIXTEEN

Being justified freely by his grace through the redemption that is in Christ Jesus: Whom God hath set forth to be a propitiation through faith in his blood, to declare his righteousness for the remission of sins that are past, through the forbearance of God; To declare, I say, at this time his righteousness: that he might be just, and the justifier of him which believeth in Jesus. Where is boasting then? It is excluded. By what law? of works? Nay: but by the law of faith. -Romans 3:24-27

As believers, it is our duty to have faith in the blood of Jesus. Our righteousness without Him is as filthy rags and there is nothing that can be done through our own endeavors to earn peace with God. His blood alone is the only thing that can cleanse us from the sin nature and the condemnation it brings. "Not by works of righteousness which we have done, but according to his mercy he saved us, by the washing of regeneration, and renewing of the Holy Ghost," Titus 3:5. There is cleansing, washing power in Jesus' blood. It can even wash your genes!

OVERCOMING THE EBOLA VIRUS

In 2015 in Liberia, there was a deadly outbreak of the Ebola disease. Reports and pictures of the effects of Ebola dominated the news, especially when it was discovered that an American missionary, Dr. Kent Brantley, fell ill to this dreaded virus. There was no known cure for Ebola at the time, and Brantley discovered his own outbreak after having cared for Liberians with Ebola.

An experimental drug, in extremely limited supply, called ZMapp was being developed, but it was a six month process. During the testing of this medicine, mice were exposed to fragments of the Ebola virus. Upon exposure, the antibodies generated within the mice's blood were harvested to created the medicine. ZMapp worked by preventing the virus from entering and infecting new cells.

An antibody is a protein, made by the body, that latches onto foreign bacteria and viruses to make them ineffective. Each antibody is designed to target and to bind a particular opponent. Effector B cells (which produce the antibodies) then clear the infection. Once cleared, these cells persist as memory cells that can survive for years or even a lifetime. In the case of ZMapp, three antibodies worked together to bind the Ebola virus.

With much prayer from his family, as well as from believers around the world, Dr. Brantley took this new treatment. After several grueling weeks of treatment, Brantley recovered and has since returned to Liberia with his family. However, before returning to Liberia, Dr. Brantley helped to save the life of an NBC cameraman, Ashoka Mukpo, who was also diagnosed with Ebola. Without hesitation, Dr. Brantley donated his once infected and now cured plasma, which was then used to save Mukpo's life. Because of Dr. Brantley's intervention, the Ebola virus was completely bound and Mukpo fully recovered. The power to overcome the deadly Ebola disease was in the blood of one man, who freely gave his blood plasma to save another.[29]

THE OVERCOMING AND CLEANSING POWER OF JESUS' BLOOD

Because of the intervening act of love and generosity of Jesus Christ on the cross, anyone who will put faith in His precious blood will receive the power to live an overcoming life. Life is in His blood. The spotless, pure blood of Jesus is our Divine "antibody" that continues to bind the effect of sin and set anyone who receives its power completely free.

Neither by the blood of goats and calves, but by his own blood he entered in once into the holy place, having obtained eternal redemption for us. For if the blood of bulls and of goats, and the ashes of an heifer sprinkling the unclean, sanctifieth to the purifying of the flesh: How much more shall the blood of Christ, who through the eternal Spirit offered himself without spot to God, purge your conscience from dead works to serve the living God? -Hebrews 9:12-14

When sin, sickness, addiction, fear, darkness, and disease come against you, just remember that as a Christian washed in the blood, you have a blessed "antibody" working on your behalf through the redemptive work of Christ Jesus. When He became sin, He took in Himself the "disease" Adam released to mankind through his disobedience. When Jesus was raised from the dead, He stepped out of the tomb as absolute master of death in all its phases; hell and all of its hosts, satan and all his works, sin and all of its consequences. He was the first of a redeemed, restored, victorious humanity that would follow. Jesus is the Firstborn from the dead; the first Man to enter death and master it. Jesus is Lord!

Jesus, the spotless Lamb of God, carried His blood through every temptation and test and came through victorious. In the garden of Gethsemane, Jesus sanctified Himself praying, "Not my will, but Thine be done." There is sanctifying power in His blood. When we apply it to any rebellion, disobedience, selfishness, or pride in our lives, there is power to overcome. You can even plead the blood of Jesus over your feelings.

The blood of Jesus carries all that Jesus is and all that He has done for us. The blood of Jesus and the

Holy Spirit are inseparable. Where the blood of Jesus is applied, in faith, the Holy Spirit makes real within us everything Jesus has done.

Now the God of peace, that brought again from the dead our Lord Jesus, that great shepherd of the sheep, through the blood of the everlasting covenant, Make you perfect in every good work to do his will, working in you that which is well pleasing in his sight, through Jesus Christ; to whom be glory for ever and ever. Amen.
-Hebrews 13:20-21

Strengthen (complete, perfect) and make you what you ought to be and equip you with everything good that you may carry out His will; [while He Himself] works in you and accomplishes that which is pleasing in His sight, through Jesus Christ (the Messiah)...
-Hebrews 13:21, Amplified

CONFESSIONS OF FAITH

1. *I have been justified with God through faith in the blood of Jesus. My sin has been remitted. I have been made righteous through faith in Jesus' blood.*

2. *Not by works of righteousness which we have done, but according to his mercy he saved us, by the washing of regeneration, and renewing of the Holy Ghost. (Titus 3:5)*

3. *Jesus has the divine antibody in His blood that has overcome sin and all the curse that sin brings. In the name of Jesus, I overcome by the blood of the Lamb and the Word of my testimony (Revelation 12:11).*

4. *I plead and apply the blood of Jesus to my mind, my feelings, emotions and my will.*

5. *I receive the sanctifying power of the blood of Jesus. God is making me perfect in every good work to do his will, working in me that which is well pleasing in his sight, through Jesus Christ; to whom be glory for ever and ever. Amen (Hebrews 13:20-21).*

God has a reputation

for taking some real losers

and making them

champions.

17

THE BLOODLINE OF A CHAMPION

CHAPTER SEVENTEEN

For whatsoever is born of God overcometh the world: and this is the victory that overcometh the world, even our faith. -1 John 5:4

American Pharaoh was the winner of the coveted 2015 Triple Crown title for thoroughbred racehorses. This extraordinary racehorse won the Kentucky Derby, Preakness, and Belmont Stakesn — a phenomenal achievement. What grabbed my attention, however, was his heritage. American Pharaoh is the great, great, great grandson of Secretariat, who was the winner of the Triple Crown in 1973. Secretariat was the beloved champion thoroughbred whose records, set forty years, ago, are still unbroken to this day. What made him outstanding was not only his physique, but also his pedigree, which he passed on to the champions in his bloodline. One of those thoroughbreds, as mentioned before, was American Pharaoh. He became the twelfth horse in this bloodline to win the Triple Crown.

It was interesting to see just how many championship racehorses were actually in Secretariat's bloodline. In fact, the top five finishers in the Kentucky Derby and all the contenders in the 2015 Preakness were descendants of Secretariat. One of his grandsons, Storm Cat, was among the preeminent stallions of his time. Storm Cat's owners had sired him 1,400 times, and there were those who were willing to pay $500,000 just to breed him once! Greatness was in his blood.

American Pharaoh shares the same characteristics as his famous great, great, great grandfather, Secretariat. One observer said about him: "He can run in the mud or on dry tracks, on the rail or to the outside, come from behind or stay in the lead." Generations later, the same championship status is in his bloodline.[30]

THE CHAMPIONSHIP PEDIGREE

In the world of championship horse breeding, the pedigree of the sire defines the value and expectation set on those in his bloodline. Likewise, Christians have been "re-fathered" by God, which puts us in the bloodline of Christ, the Firstborn from the dead. Jesus' pedigree is one of complete victory in every area of life. Jesus won in three places: hell, Heaven, and the heart of the believer. He triumphed over HELL and all of the devil's works; His blood has opened Heaven and gives us boldness in the very presence of God. It reaches into the HEARTS of believers and removes the guilt and stain of sin. The blood of Jesus purges our conscious and silences the voice of self-condemnation.

Jesus Christ is the greatest champion of all time. His Name is famous. He overcame tremendous adversity, rejection, betrayal, crucifixion, and even death. If you have been born of God, you are an overcomer with His pedigree. You should never say, "I'm only human." Instead, because you share Christ's bloodline, you should say, "I'm also human." God has a reputation for taking some real losers and making them champions!

But ye are a chosen generation, a royal priesthood, an holy nation, a peculiar people; that ye should shew forth the praises of him who hath called you out of darkness into his marvelous light. -1 Peter 2:9

You are a show-stock people. -Jordan

Therefore if any man be in Christ, he is a new creature: old things are passed away; behold, all things are become new. -2 Corinthians 5:17

YOU ARE VALUABLE: PURCHASED WITH PRECIOUS BLOOD

Forasmuch as ye know that ye were not redeemed with corruptible things, as silver and gold, from your vain conversation received by tradition from your fathers; But with the precious blood of Christ, as of a lamb without blemish and without spot. -1 Peter 1:18,19

The value placed on a thoroughbred colt is high due to the price paid to breed him in a championship bloodline. We are valuable because of the high price

Jesus paid to redeem us. Jesus' precious blood was the payment to bring us into CHAMPIONSHIP STATUS. We are a new breed, born to win in His Name (2 Corinthians 5:17). "And from Jesus Christ, who is the faithful witness, and the first begotten of the dead, and the prince of the kings of the earth. Unto him that loved us, and washed us from our sins in his own blood, And hath made us kings and priests unto God and his Father; to him be glory and dominion forever and ever. Amen," Revelations 1:5-6. In Jesus' bloodline, we have the power to overcome sin (1 John 3:9). Sin's dominion has been broken. We are loved, blood washed, and made kings and priests unto God. We are always triumphant in Christ Jesus (2 Corinthians 2:14).

EXERCISE FAITH IN
THE BLOOD OF JESUS

More knowledge concerning the blood of Jesus will increase our faith (Romans 3:25 and Romans 10:17). Faith in His blood explodes when we know what it has done for us, what it purchased for us, and what it will do in us.

> *"Faith is largely dependent on knowledge. If knowledge of what the blood can accomplish is not accurate, then faith expects little, and the more powerful effects of the blood are limited. Feeble ideas of its power prevent the deeper and more perfect manifestations of its effects."* [31]
>
> *-Andrew Murray*

Through increased faith in the blood of Jesus, the Church will rise to defeat the powers of darkness. This is the victory that overcomes the world. Remember this: what was true about the great Secretariat and his descendants is true about every person who has been born of God: "You can run in the mud or on dry tracks, on the rail or to the outside, come from behind or stay in the lead." ***You are in the Bloodline of the Champion. You are in the Bloodline of Jesus Christ!***

Footnotes

1.   Page 21, *The Holy Spirit, My Senior Partner. Dr. Yonggi Cho*

2.   Page 36, *Healing the Sick. TL Osborn*

3.   Page 39, *Healing From Heaven. Lilian B. Yeomans*

4.   Page 46, *Christ, the Healer. FF Bosworth*

5.   Page 49, *Christ, the Healer. FF Bosworth*

6.   Page 60, *Strong's Concordance, "homologia"*

7.   Page 65, *"O For a Thousand Tongues to Sing." Charles Wesley*

8.   Page 65, *Strong's Concordance, "thanks"*

9.   Page 67, *Two Kinds of Faith. E.W. Kenyon*

10. Page 67, *Christ, the Healer. FF Bosworth*

11. Page 67, *Kenneth E. Hagin*

12. Page 68, *Christ, the Healer. FF Bosworth*

13. Page 68, *Two Kinds of Faith. E.W. Kenyon*

14. Page 68, *Two Kinds of Faith. E.W. Kenyon*

15. Page 68, *Christ, the Healer. FF Bosworth*

16. Page 68, *Two Kinds of Faith. E.W. Kenyon*

17. Page 68, *Christ, the Healer. FF Bosworth*

18. Page 72, *Healing from Heaven. Lilian B. Yeoman.*

19. Page 78, *How Things Work. Brain Marshall*

20. Page 78, *New Testament Greek Lexicon. "Dunamis"*

21. Page 83, *Strong's Concordance. "euangelion"*

22. Page 95, *New Testament Words. William Barclay*

23. Page 99, *The Forth Dimension. David Yonggi Cho*

24. Page 104, *The Power of Positive Thinking. Norman Vincent Peale*

25. Page108, *Bible Doctrines. PC Nelson*

26. Page 115, *The Power of Positive Thinking. Norman Vincent Peale*

27. Page 118, *merriam-webster.com. "Meditate"*

28. Page 118, *merriam-webster.com. "Cogitate"*

29. Page 136, *www.cbsnews.com. "Inside Story of the First Two Ebola Patients"*

30. Page 142, *vafarmbureau.org. "American Pharoah"*

31. Page 146, *The Power of the Blood. Andrew Murray*

References

Amplified Bible. Zondervan Publishing House, Grand Rapids, Michigan, 1972. (AMP)

Barclay, William. The New Testament, A New Translation. Collins, London, England, 1968.

Barclay, William. New Testament Words. The Westminster Press, Philadelphia, Pennsylvania, 1964.

Bosworth, F.F. (1994). Christ, the Healer. Fleming H. Revell Company

Brain, Marshall (2010). How Things Work, Chartwell Books.

Burer, Michael and Miller, Jeffrey (2008). A New Reader's Lexicon of the Greek New Testament. Kregel Academic & Professional

Cho, Yonggi, (1996). Holy Spirit, My Senior Partner: Understanding the Holy Spirit and His Gifts. Charisma House.

Cho, Yonggi, (1979). The Forth Dimension. Bridge-Logos Publishers.

Common English Bible. Nashville, Tennessee, 2011. Concordant Literal New Testament, Sixth Edition. Concordant Publishing Concern, 1976. (CEB)

Contemporary English Version. American Bible Society. New York, NK, 1995. (CEV)

Cornish, Gerald Warre. Saint Paul from the Trenches. Spirit to Spirit Publications, Tulsa, Oklahoma, 1981.

Doddridge, P. The Family Expositor: or a Paraphrase and Version of the New Testament. C & J Rivington, London England, 1828.

Doswell. "Secretariat Scion American Pharoah Trying for Triple Crown." Secretariat Scion American Pharoah Trying for Triple Crown. Farm Bureau - Virginia, 21 May 2015. Web. 01 June 2016.

Firgir, Jessica. "Inside Story of the First Two U.S. Ebola Patients." Www.cbs.com. N.p., 13 Nov. 2014. Web. 1 June 2016.

References cont'd.

Glaser, Carl (1828). O for a Thousand to Sing. http://www.cyberhymnal.org/htm/o/ f/o/ofor1000.htm.

Hahn, Nick. "American Pharoah Has Triple Crown Lineage." Richmond Times-Dispatch. Richmond Times-Dispatch, 4 June 2015. Web. 01 June 2016. <http://www. richmond.com/sports/article_a21c617d-99c6-5be3-9377-3701fb02f262.html>.

Johnson, Ben Campbell. The Heart of Paul, A Rational Paraphrase of the New Testament. Word Books, Waco, Texas, 1976.

Jordan, Clarence. The Cotton Patch Version of Paul's Epistles. Association Press, New York, New York, 1968.

Kenyon, E.W. (1989). Two Kinds of Faith. Kenyons Gospel Publishing.

Laubach, Frank C. The Inspired Letters in Clearest English. Thomas Nelson and Sons, New York, New York, 1956.

Lillian B. Yeomans, M. (2003). Healing from Heaven. Springfield, MO: Gospel Publishing House.

Lovett, C.S. Lovett's Lights on Galatians, Ephesians, Philippians, Colossians, 1 & 2 Thessalonians with Rephrased Text. Personal Christianity, Baldwin Park, California, 1969.

Maron, Dina Fine. "Ebola Doctor Reveals How Infected Americans Were Cured." Scientific American. Scientific American, 27 Aug. 2014. Web. 01 June 2016.

Merriam Webster. Merriam Webster, n.d. Web. 01 June 2016. <http://www.merriam-webster.com/>.

Moffatt, James. The Holy Bible Containing the Old and New Testament. Double Day Dora & Company, Inc., New York, 1926. (MOF)

Montgomery, Helen Barrett. Centenary Translation of the New Testament. The American Baptist Publication Society, Philadelphia, Pennsylvania, 1924.

Murray, Andrew, (1993). Power of the Blood. Christian Literature Crusade.

References cont'd.

Nelson, PC (2012). Bible Doctrines. Publishing House.

New Living Translation. Tyndale House Publishers. Wheaton, Illinois, 1996. (NLT)

Osborn, T.L. (1986). Healing The Sick. Harrison House.

Peale, Norman Vincent, (2003). The Power of Positive Thinking. Touchstone;

Peterson, Eugene. The Messages//Remix, The Bible in Contempory Language. NavPress Publishing Group, Colorado Springs, Colorado, 2003. (MSG)

Strong, James. The New Strong Exhaustive Concordance of the Bible,

Taylor, John. A Paraphrase with Notes on the Epistles to the Romans. J. Waugh, London, England, 1974.

Taylor, Ken. The Living Bible. Tyndale House Publishers, Wheaton, Illinois, 1971. (TLB)

The Bible in Basic English. University Press, Cambridge, England, 1965.

The Translator's New Testament. The British and Foreign Bible Society, London, England, 1977. (TRANS)

The Jerusalem Bible. Double Day and Company, Inc., New York, New York, 1968. (JER)

Wade, G.W. The Documents of the New Testament. Thomas Burby and Company, London, England, 1934.

Wigglesworth, S. (2001). Ever Increasing Faith. New Kensington, PA: Whitaker House.

Wood, C.T. The Life, Letters and Religion of St. Paul. T. & T. Clark, Edinburgh, England, n.d.

Wuest, Kenneth S. The New Testament, An Expanded Translation. William B. Eerdmans Publishing Company, Grand Rapids, Michigan, 1981.

About the Author

Mark and Trina Hankins travel nationally and internationally preaching the Word of God with the power of the Holy Spirit. Their message centers on the spirit of faith, who the believer is in Christ, and the work of the Holy Spirit.

After over 40 years of pastoral and traveling ministry, Mark and Trina are now ministering full-time in campmeetings, leadership conferences, and church services across the United States and around the world. Their son Aaron and his wife Errin Cody are now the pastors of Christian Worship Center in Alexandria, Louisiana. Their daughter Alicia Moran and her husband Caleb pastor Metro Life Church in Lafayette, Louisiana. Mark and Trina have eight grandchildren.

Mark is the author of several books. For more information on Mark Hankins Ministries, please log on to our website, www.markhankins.org.

Acknowledgments

Special thanks to:

My wife Trina.

My son, Aaron and his wife Errin Cody; their daughters, Avery Jane and Macy Claire; their son, Jude Aaron.

My daughter Alicia and her husband Caleb; their sons, Jaiden Mark, Gavin Luke, Landon James, and Dylan Paul; their daughter Hadley Marie.

My parents, Pastor B.B. and Velma Hankins, who are now in Heaven with the Lord.

My wife's parents, Rev. William and Ginger Behrman.

Mark Hankins Ministries

PO BOX 12863 ALEXANDRIA, LA 71315

Phone: 318.767.2001   E-mail: contact@markhankins.org

Visit us on the web: www.markhankins.org

Mark Hankins Ministries Publications

SPIRIT-FILLED SCRIPTURE STUDY GUIDE

A comprehensive study of scriptures in over 120 different translations on topics such as: Redemption, Faith, Finances, Prayer and many more.

THE BLOODLINE OF A CHAMPION - THE POWER OF THE BLOOD OF JESUS

The blood of Jesus is the liquid language of love that flows from the heart of God & gives us hope in all circumstances. In this book, you will clearly see what the blood has done FOR US but also what the blood has done IN US as believers.

TAKING YOUR PLACE IN CHRIST

Many Christians talk about what they are trying to be and what they are going to be. This book is about who you are NOW as believers in Christ.

PAUL'S SYSTEM OF TRUTH

Paul's System of Truth reveals man's redemption in Christ, the reality of what happened from the cross to the throne and how it is applied for victory in life through Jesus Christ.

THE SECRET POWER OF JOY

If you only knew what happens in the Spirit when you rejoice, you would rejoice everyday. Joy is one of the great secrets of faith. This book will show you the importance of the joy of the Lord in a believer's life.

11:23 – THE LANGUAGE OF FAITH

Never under-estimate the power of one voice. Over 100 inspirational, mountain-moving quotes to "stir up" the spirit of faith in you.

LET THE GOOD TIMES ROLL

This book focuses on the five key factors to Heaven on earth: The Holy Spirit, Glory, Faith, Joy, and Redemption. The Holy Spirit is a genius. If you will listen to Him, He will make you look smart.

THE POWER OF IDENTIFICATION WITH CHRIST

Learn how God identified us with Christ in His death, burial, resurrection, and seating in Heaven. The same identical life, victory, joy, and blessings that are In Christ are now in you. This is the glory and the mystery of Christianity – the power of the believer's identification with Christ.

REVOLUTIONARY REVELATION

This book provides excellent insight on how the spirit of wisdom and revelation is mandatory for believers to access their call, inheritance, and authority in Christ.

GOD'S HEALING WORD by Trina Hankins

Trina's testimony and a practical guide to receiving healing through meditating on the Word of God. This guide includes: testimonies, practical teaching, Scriptures & confessions, and a CD with Scriptures & confessions (read by Mark Hankins).